Family Life
in the U.S.A.

THEN & NOW

Maya Franklin

Table of Contents

Not So Different

Long ago in colonial times, people lived and worked in cities, towns, and the country. Children studied, did chores, and played when they could. Families ate meals together and went to church together. They took care of each other.

Colonial times are the times before the United States became a country, when people were trying to build a life far away from their home countries in Europe.

3

That is a lot like families today.
Families then and now are not so
different from each other. They are the
same in the most important ways, like
caring for and loving each other. But
they are different in some ways, too.

Homes *Then*

Keeping Babies Warm
Babies were kept in their cradles near the fireplace to keep them warm.

Family homes were small and built close together for safety. Even farmers built their homes near town.

Whole families lived together. Mothers, fathers, brothers, sisters, grandparents, aunts, uncles, and cousins often shared one house!

House floors were made of wood or dirt. Windows were small. The only light came from the sun, candles, and the fireplace.

A large fireplace was used for warmth and cooking. Hooks and poles with pots and pans covered the fireplace.

Necessaries

Toilets back then were in small buildings away from the house. They were called "necessaries."

There was little furniture, and the men and boys in a family usually made it.

The family sat on benches. The table was a board placed across barrels. Small boards called trenchers were used for plates, and people ate with their hands or spoons. They slept on featherbeds. They used washing bowls to clean themselves. Trunks and cupboards were used to store things.

Homes *Now*

Today family members live both near and far. Telephones keep people in touch even when they are far away.

Floors are usually made of cement or rough wood and covered with wood, tile, or carpet. Windows are large. Lights are everywhere. Fireplaces may be used for heat, but most homes have heaters or furnaces for warmth and stoves for cooking.

Most furniture is bought from stores. Families eat at all sorts of tables. They sometimes use their hands, but forks, knives, and spoons are used, too.

Mattresses are usually stuffed with foam and springs. Bathrooms are inside the house. Closets, cupboards, and shelves are used to store things.

Families come in many sizes. Many different kinds of people make a family. A family might have just two people or more than a dozen.

Every home is different, but no matter the size, a family is still a family.

Adults *Then*

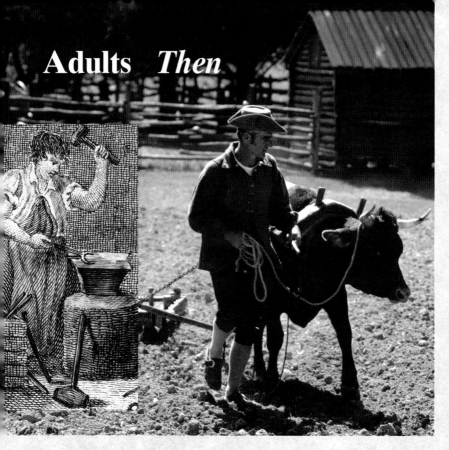

Adults worked hard from sunrise to sundown. Many men were farmers. They cared for crops and animals, made repairs, and provided food for their families.

Women cared for the homes and children. They prepared food. They cleaned, sewed, and spun thread.

At sixteen, children became adults. Girls married and ran their own houses. Boys paid taxes and served in the **militia**.

A **militia** (me-LISH-e) is like an army that is called to duty during emergencies. Today we call such groups the National Guard or the Army Reserves.

13

Adults *Now*

Adults today work hard, too, but usually not for so long. They have days off and vacations. Stores and inventions make life easier, too. For example, most people buy food and clothes at stores. Dishwashers, cars, and microwaves save time and trouble.

Some adults work away from home and spend the rest of the time with their families. Others work at home and take care of their families in that way.

Sixteen-year-olds are still children, but they can do some adult things like driving and having a job. They usually do not get married. They are too young for the army, but if they have jobs, they pay taxes!

Children *Then*

An **apprentice** (u-PREN-tis) is someone who learns about a job such as blacksmithing or carpentry by working with an adult who already does that job.

Boys did chores, went to school if there was one, and studied. A boy could become an **apprentice** when he was eight.

Cooking

Cooking then was hard to do. Girls had to learn to do things like grind wheat, skin meat, measure flour with just their hands, and test the oven temperature by sticking their hand and arm inside for ten seconds. If they got burned, it was too hot to bake bread and pies!

Don't Be Lazy!

Children then could not be lazy or complain. If they got tired, they could not show it. Everyone had to work hard to do his or her part. Even young children had chores like pulling feathers from geese to stuff the beds.

Girls stayed busy, too, but they usually did not attend school. Instead, they learned to be housewives. Even little girls learned to sew, cook, and clean.

Breeches are pants that go just below the knee. **Petticoats** are skirts, and girls often wore several at once. Babies also wore puddings, or soft pillows around their middles to keep them safe if they fell.

Young boys and girls usually wore long gowns. At six, they began to wear clothes exactly like their parents wore. Boys wore **breeches** and vests. Girls wore **petticoats** and aprons.

Children did not have much time for play. When their work was done, they played with simple toys they made themselves like hoops, kites, and dolls. They played hopscotch and cat's cradle or built houses from corncobs.

Children *Now*

Most Popular Names

Boys *Then*	Boys *Now*
Matthew	Jacob
John	Michael
William	Joshua
Edward	Matthew
Thomas	Nicholas

Girls *Then*	Girls *Now*
Sarah	Sarah
Hannah	Hannah
Mary	Ashley
Abigail	Emily
Charity	Samantha

Boys and girls today go to school. They have chores, too, but usually not as many as children did long ago.

Children today play much of the
time, and they have all sorts of toys.
Parents now know that playtime is
important for children.

Comparison Chart

Family life is different in many ways today from what it was long ago. But many things are the same, too.

Read this chart. Which way is most like your family?

Then	Now
Whole families live together.	Families come in many different sizes, with different people.
Families make their own clothes.	Most families buy their clothes.
Families grow and hunt for their food.	Most families buy their food.
Families make the furniture.	Most families buy their furniture from stores.
The toilet is outside the house.	The toilet is inside the house.

Then	Now
Families use washing bowls to clean themselves.	Families use sinks, showers, and tubs to clean themselves.
Women work only in the home.	Women work in or out of the home.
People work as long as there is daylight.	People work the hours they need and take time off.
People become adults at sixteen.	People are still children at sixteen.
Only boys go to school, if there is one.	Girls and boys go to school.
Children play only if there is time.	Children play much of the time.
Children under six wear gowns.	Children under six usually wear clothes like older children.
Children six and older dress exactly like their parents.	Children wear children's clothing, which is sometimes like their parents.

Glossary

apprentice   a young person who learns a job from an adult who already does that job

breeches   pants that go just below the knee

cat's cradle   a child's game played with string formed in different positions around the hands

colonial times   the times before the United States became a country, when people were trying to build a life far away from their home countries in Europe

family   a group of people who live together who are usually related to each other; families are most often parents and children

family life   how a family lives, works, and plays

fireplace   a stone or brick structure used for setting fires for warmth, light, or cooking

furniture   items inside a house used for sitting, sleeping, and storing things

hopscotch   a game played by jumping on one or two feet through a pattern on the ground

militia   a group like an army that is called to duty during emergencies

petticoats   skirts

taxes   money paid to the government to run cities, states, and the country

trencher   a plate made of a small, wood board